daughters, S
divorced. His
wife, Patricia
1937), was disa... continued

devoted to Hilda for the rest of his life, even writing letters to her after her death. He was elected as an Associate of the Royal Academy the year the Burghclere paintings were finished, but he resigned three years later, not rejoining until 1950.

The chapel spawned the idea for a sequel, the *Church of Me*, which was designed to be the setting for his large-scale celebratory cycles of sacred and erotic art. Although he painted some pieces intended for it, the chapel itself was never realised. His *Shipbuilding on the Clyde* series, set in Port Glasgow, and painted whilst he was Official War Artist during World War II, was perhaps the most obvious conceptual heir to Sandham, but again it lacked its own 'temple'.

In 1959 Spencer returned to live in his childhood home, the same year that he was knighted, but also that in which he succumbed to the cancer that had afflicted him.

in 1927, at which time the fabric of the chapel had been completed. From then on, until 1932, his life was consumed primarily by Burghclere, although during this time his personal life was chequered. In 1925 he married his first wife, Hilda Carline, with whom he had two

*Above* Travoys with
Wounded Soldiers arriving
at a Dressiong Station at
Smol, Macedonia, 1919
(Imperial War Museum)

*Right* The Resurrection,
Cookham, 1924–7 (Tate)

# Spencer and the Great War

## Beaufort War Hospital

Spencer's diminutive stature did not lend itself to hand-to-hand combat in the trenches. However, he felt conflicted: 'I think it is necessary for people like me to join … the one great drawback to our joining is our mother.' His brothers Percy and Sydney had enlisted, but initially Stanley made do with military training in the Maidenhead Civic Guard and St John's Ambulance classes. Having left his early masterpiece *Swan Upping* (Tate) unfinished, he enlisted in the Royal Army Medical Corps, and was promptly enrolled as a medical orderly at Beaufort War Hospital in Bristol (an asylum that had been commandeered as a hospital) in the autumn of 1915. 'It seems such rotten luck that Gil [his brother] and I had to do this instead of being "tommies"', Spencer had claimed. As soon as he arrived there, he felt that 'all my patriotic ardour, which I had struggled hard to retain, seemed again to leave me. A great clammy death seemed to be sitting on all my desires and hopes.' Spencer was the lowest of the low in the working hierarchy, and spent his days fetching, carrying, scrubbing and scouring.

Spencer sought solace in areas of quiet, between the bath tubs, or in cupboards; places where he could read his art books. His outlook was transformed by an encounter with Desmond Chute, whose visit Stanley compared to 'Christ visiting Hell.' Chute gave Stanley a copy of St Augustine's *Confessions*, which taught Spencer to find God and solace

' … bearing, filling, coming, going, fetching, carrying, sorting, opening doors, shutting them, carrying tea-urns, scrubbing floors.'
Spencer celebrated the mundane aspects of hospital life.

in everyday tasks and routine. It is arguably this philosophy, being 'ever busy … yet ever at rest', that informed Spencer's paintings in the chapel.

Above A ward in Beaufort War Hospital with Spencer standing on the far left, marked as 'me', 1915 (Glenside Museum, Bristol)

A souvenir guide

# Stanley Spencer at Burghclere

## The Oratory of All Souls Sandham Memorial Chapel

### Hampshire

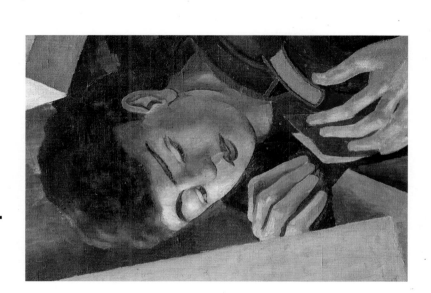

**National Trust**

# 'A Symphony in Rashers of Bacon'

Sandham Memorial Chapel (originally dedicated as the Oratory of All Souls) is a monument not only to a soldier who had served in the Great War, but also to the genius of an artist who had served on the same front, in Macedonia.

Undoubtedly, it is the spirit and personality of that artist, Sir Stanley Spencer (1891–1959), which dominate the whole. Lt Harry Sandham, to whom the chapel is dedicated, barely features, save in the plaque by the door that bears his name. The concept was entirely Spencer's, the murals inside detailing his everyday experiences during the war. He called it a 'symphony in rashers of bacon' with a 'tea-making obligato', and for him the mundane became infused with a spirituality that helped him endure the grim reality of working as a hospital orderly and on the front in Macedonia. Although the soldiers that appear in his murals neither smile, nor engage the viewer, Spencer was insistent that it was a 'happy place'.

Spencer was lucky enough to find benefactors, John Louis and (Phyllis) Mary Behrend, who were sufficiently well-off and forbearing to support his grandiose scheme. The result is an austere casket with a jewel-like interior, sometimes overwhelming in its wealth of detail and depth of vision. It is unique in English art history, not only for the images themselves, but also the singular dynamic between artist and patron, and the bravery of them all.

'They don't look like war pictures … they rather look like Heaven, a place I am becoming very familiar with.'

Stanley Spencer

Above Cooking rashers of bacon in a mess tin; detail from *Camp at Karasuli* (18)

THESE PAINTINGS BY
STANLEY SPENCER
AND THIS ORATORY
ARE THE FULFILMENT
OF A DESIGN WHICH
HE CONCEIVED
WHILST ON
ACTIVE
SERVICE
1914-1918

# Genesis of the chapel

While recovering from malaria in Salonika in October 1918, Spencer wrote to his sister Florence, 'When I come home I am going to learn fresco painting and then … we are going to build a church … if I don't do this on earth, I will do it in Heaven.' During a trip to Yugoslavia with the Carline family he started to make detailed drawings for this scheme of war paintings. These plans were further realised on the dining room table of his friend, the artist Henry Lamb (1883–1960), at his house in Dorset. In the summer of 1923 Lamb described how Spencer sat all day 'evolving acres of Salonika and Bristol war compositions'. It was at this time that Lamb invited his patrons, John Louis and Mary Behrend (whom Spencer had met before the war), to visit. Seeing Spencer's sketches pinned to the wall, they became determined to build 'this castle in the sky', somewhat to the chagrin of Henry Lamb, who had hoped to benefit from his patrons' visit himself. When Spencer got the commission, he had exclaimed, 'What ho, Giotto!' – in recognition of the Italian artist whose painted Arena Chapel in Padua had inspired his. For the Behrends, the artistic impetus was Spencer's own, and it was very much his project: 'It infuriates us to see it [the chapel] as having been commissioned … he had this thing complete in his head for so many years …

the whole thing was his idea.' Spencer had wanted his chapel to be built in his home village of Cookham, but the Behrends insisted that it be situated in their own village, Burghclere, in Hampshire. They struggled and failed to find financial help for the building of the chapel itself, and so it fell to these modest collectors to fund Spencer's dream in its entirety.

Above Giotto's Arena Chapel in Padua was the inspiration for the Sandham Memorial Chapel

Below Study for the north wall, 1923 (Stanley Spencer Gallery). Spencer produced numerous studies for the chapel

Above Stanley Spencer, painted by his friend Henry Lamb in 1928 (National Portrait Gallery)

Stanley Spencer was born and grew up in Cookham, Berkshire – a cocooned existence which informed the essence of his being and his art for the rest of his life. The Spencers were not a wealthy family, but were cultured, teaching their children the value of music and literature. These two pastimes remained central to Spencer and his artistic outlook; his daughters have noted that the Sandham paintings are themselves like one of Bach's

Fugues. His artistic career began in 1907 at Maidenhead Technical School, which was not far from his home, Fernlea. It was his father who filled in his application form for the Slade School of Art, which he attended between 1908 and 1912, and where he was nicknamed 'Cookham' for his daily commute back home. He took no lessons in oil painting, instead studying draughtsmanship under Prof. Henry Tonks, himself a renowned artist. Stanley soon became recognised as one of the stellar students in a brilliant generation that included C.R.W. Nevinson, William Roberts, David Bomberg, Paul Nash and Dora Carrington.

Spencer's greatest work arguably came out of his experiences serving in the Great War (see p.6). He returned to England full of hope: 'I felt, on returning home, as if I were performing a miracle every time I beheld the familiar spots'. However, he was devastated to learn of the loss of his brother, Sydney, who had been killed in the last few months of the war. He had proclaimed, 'It is not proper or sensible to expect to paint well after such experiences', but, having been appointed a War Artist, he painted for the Ministry of Information *Travoys with Wounded Soldiers Arriving at a Dressing Station at Smol, Macedonia* (1919; Imperial War Museum), which, like the Burghclere paintings, was 'not a scene of horror, but a scene of redemption'.

Spencer did not start painting the Burghclere panels until he had finished *The Resurrection, Cookham* (Tate; started 1924),

exemplary bravery in action, standing by his officer when wounded.

Malaria was also one of the main enemies facing soldiers on the Macedonian front. It was whilst hospitalised for malaria in October 1918 that Stanley learnt that the Bulgarians had called for an armistice. He returned home in December that year and was shocked to find 'how little my Faith has stood in my stead to help me.' The concept of a personal God became complicated for Spencer: for him, the joy of religion and God was found in Biblical narrative and the everyday things that he loved.

*Left Detail of Riverbed at Todorovo (19)*

*Below Detail of Kit Inspection (5)*

## Tweseldown and Salonika

Spencer left Bristol on 12 May 1916 for training and eventual mobilisation at Tweseldown in Surrey. This was 'great fun after "ward" work'. It was only when he was finally at sea that he learned he was destined for Salonika. His reading of Homer had inspired him and he revelled in the journey there, which became like an Odyssey flooded with new landscapes and mythical surroundings. He was assigned to the 68th Field Ambulance, where he worked as an orderly, transferring the wounded to mule-drawn travoys. The grim reality of war soon hit home.

In October 1917 Spencer was transferred to the 7th Battalion of the Royal Berkshires. This meant active service at the front, and by February 1918 he had written to his sister Florence that he was waiting to 'go up to the line.' He bore no grudge towards the Bulgarians, whom he was fighting; he did not want to be an instrument of death, as he 'felt a bond of universal brotherhood'. Stanley was essentially Pacifist in outlook, but he showed

# The patrons
# John Louis and Mary Behrend

When John Louis and Mary Behrend decided to build Spencer's 'castle in the sky', they were already established patrons of the Modern British art scene. Both their London house and country residence, Grey House, at Burghclere, were filled with pictures by Henry Lamb, Mark Gertler, Victor Pasmore, Edward Burra and

Augustus John. However, they were not as wealthy as the extent of their collection might suggest. The Behrends had made their money primarily from dealing in cotton seed in Egypt, chartering ships on the Baltic Exchange in London, and milling rice, but John Louis had been disinherited for marrying a gentile.

Left Henry Lamb's 1927 portrait of the Behrend family reveals their love of music (Brighton and Hove Museums)

Building the chapel cost them £8000, and that did not include payments to Spencer for his paintings; even Spencer realised that they were only comfortably well-off. When one day a formidable woman who came to look around the chapel said to him, 'It smells of money here, doesn't it?', he answered, 'No, only courage.'

The Behrends had a genuine interest in the creative process and forged a complex yet close relationship with Spencer. They were a source of friendship and support – both financial and moral – to numerous artists throughout their lives. The composer Benjamin Britten used Grey House as a place of quiet refuge, and during the Second World War the Ballet Rambert was, for a short time, also put up there.

The highly acclaimed embroiderer Madeleine Clifton was a long-term friend, who created the altar frontal for the chapel. Embellished with words from *The Tempest* and the New Testament (John 2:25), it is a deceptively modest piece, of powerful spirituality. The silverware on the altar was commissioned from W. Herbert Durst of the Casa Guidi workshops in Florence, but the nineteenth-century altar cross, inlaid with mother of pearl, was a gift, donated by Lord Justice Slesser, who was not only a close friend of the Behrends, but also a patron of Spencer.

Over the years, the Behrends' art collection was gradually sold off. Money was tight and not sufficient to maintain the fabric of the chapel, so in 1947 it was given, with an endowment, to the National Trust. It was an extraordinarily enlightened and generous gift, typical of the donors.

## Harry Sandham (1876–1920)

Once the chapel had been built, it became apparent to the Behrends that it needed a broader purpose and meaning. The political and economic climate was such that the world at large would not have looked kindly upon a chapel built solely as a temple to artistic endeavour. It was therefore dedicated to Mary Behrend's brother, Harry Sandham, who is referenced only in a baroque plaque – detested by Spencer – within the chapel.

Little is known of Harry (or 'Hal') Sandham. He enlisted in the Army Service Corps as a private in 1915, and was assigned to the Motor Transport Company as a driver. He served on the Western Front in France, but, like Spencer, he was posted to Macedonia in late 1916 and suffered from bouts of malaria. He returned home in December 1919, but fell ill on 8 March 1920. His death certificate states that he died of a ruptured spleen, although history relates that this was linked to an illness contracted whilst at war, and that it was his sister, Mary, who inadvertently administered a fatal dose of brandy.

# The building

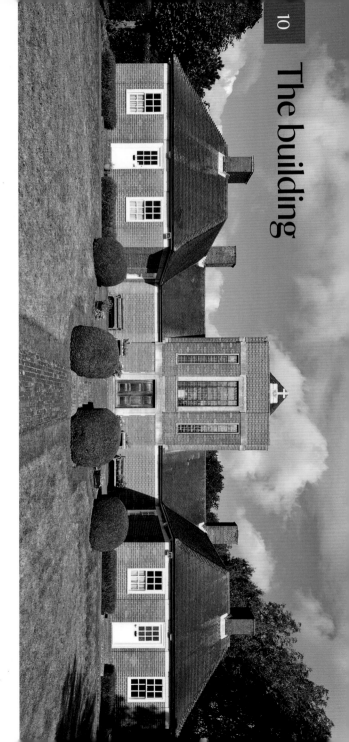

Above The Sandham Memorial Chapel is flanked by almshouses

Below A sketch by Spencer for the chapel

The Behrends had initially proposed a temporary structure to house the paintings, but Spencer declined this offer, demanding a more permanent building that would function as a chapel, rather than the secular memorial that the Behrends had wanted. The plot of land was bought from the Highclere estate of the 6th Earl of Carnarvon in 1923.

John Louis had, in the first instance, commissioned the architect George Kennedy to build the chapel, which included a narthex (or outer porch), but this was considered too fussy by Spencer. This conflict led to a public row outside the Behrends' London home, after which Kennedy never spoke to them again. In 1924, the commission to create Spencer's 'holy box' fell to Lionel Pearson, architect of the memorial to the Royal Artillery in Hyde Park. Spencer wrote that '[his] own ideas about the building are the best; that it ought to be plain outside, just like a box, and that there ought to be no … architectural ornament or features whatever.' Spencer wrote to his sister, Florence: 'I have decided the proportions of everything: length of building, height of roof, kind of tiles, height of dado and cornice,

projection of moulding of arches, size and place of window and door, so that the architect only has to make a builder's drawing from my measurements.' The relationship between patron, architect and artist was not an easy one, with a conflict between artistic vision and budget. Moreover, Spencer's artistic visualisation of space did not always translate architecturally, resulting in numerous uneasy compromises. The dado became a notable source of contention, resulting in scores of illustrated letters, some of which are in the National Trust archive. The Behrends also insisted on the addition of two almshouses, which would serve a philanthropic purpose but would also accommodate a chapel warden who could stoke the boiler. The resulting complex is eclectic and austere and came to be referred to as the 'biscuit factory' by the Behrends' children. The building was dedicated by the Bishop of Guildford on the Feast Day of the Annunciation, 25 March 1927. Neither Spencer nor the wider Behrend family attended, due to their religious views.

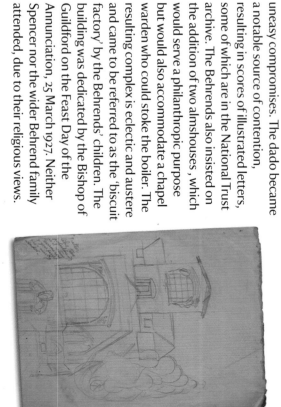

# The garden

The formal lines of the chapel are softened by the informal planting in the garden, which was influenced by the contemporary Arts and Crafts style. Naïve cottage garden plantings were combined with topiary and more formal layouts, all combined with high-quality craftsmanship and the use of local materials. The rustic well-head provides a visual focus, but was also a practical necessity for the inhabitants of the almshouses. The well was dug and built by Bill Head, who was responsible for constructing the chapel in its entirety.

To the rear of the chapel was the site of two cottage gardens, long since destroyed. To commemorate the centenary of the outbreak of the Great War, this site has been used to create a new garden, designed by Daniel Lobb and funded by a grant from the Heritage Lottery Fund. The volunteers who helped create this vision came from a wealth of diverse backgrounds, including wounded soldiers from Tedworth House, A-level students from Sparsholt College, homeless clients from St Mungo's, clients from Thrive (a horticultural therapy charity), and Sandham's own garden volunteers.

Right The new garden behind the chapel

# The Chapel Paintings

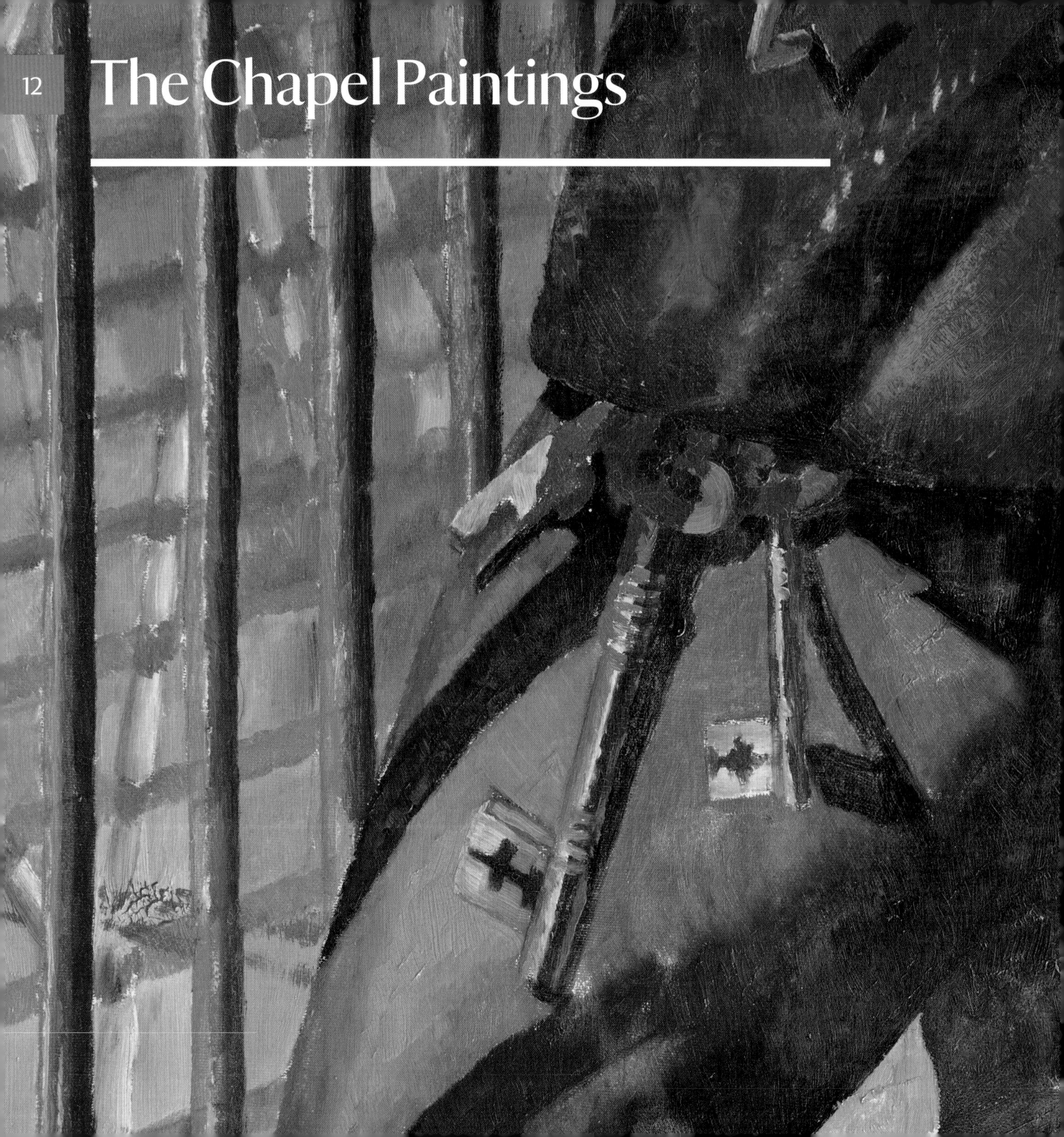

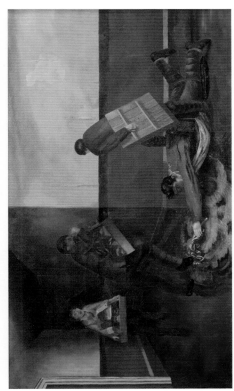

## 1 Convoy Arriving with the Wounded

The first picture of the sequence (which does not follow a narrative) shows the gate-keepers opening the iron gates to Beaufort Hospital in Bristol, described by Spencer as 'as high and massive as the gate of Hell'. He particularly liked the white triangular slings on the wounded soldiers' arms. He also recalled that they exchanged souvenirs or examined bullet holes in their helmets to escape boredom. Spencer made two references to Burghclere in the painting: the rhododendrons lining the road were common in the area; and one of the keys hanging from the gate-keeper's belt is similar to that still used to open the chapel. The high viewpoint gives us a good vantage point from which to survey the scene. This was one of the first pictures to be painted in the chapel itself. It sets the tone for the whole cycle: the human companionship of war.

## 2 Scrubbing the Floor

This painting shows Beaufort Hospital at its most institutional, with long soulless corridors, and paint peeling off the walls. Stanley wrote a letter to Richard Carline in 1929 describing the man leaning against the wall 're-adjusting the loaves of bread on his tray, before he continues his journey with it to the ward'. Spencer made various studies for the soap suds on the floor, and their painterly effect here is particularly masterful. The figure with his back to us is probably one of the asylum inmates, nicknamed 'Deborah', with whom Spencer was particularly fascinated. This is one of the first pictures, painted in Henry Lamb's studio in Hampstead in 1927.

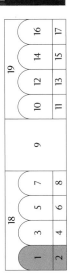

| 18 | | | | 19 | | | |
|---|---|---|---|---|---|---|---|
| 1 | 3 | 5 | 7 | 9 | 10 | 12 | 14 | 16 |
| 2 | 4 | 6 | 8 | | 11 | 13 | 15 | 17 |

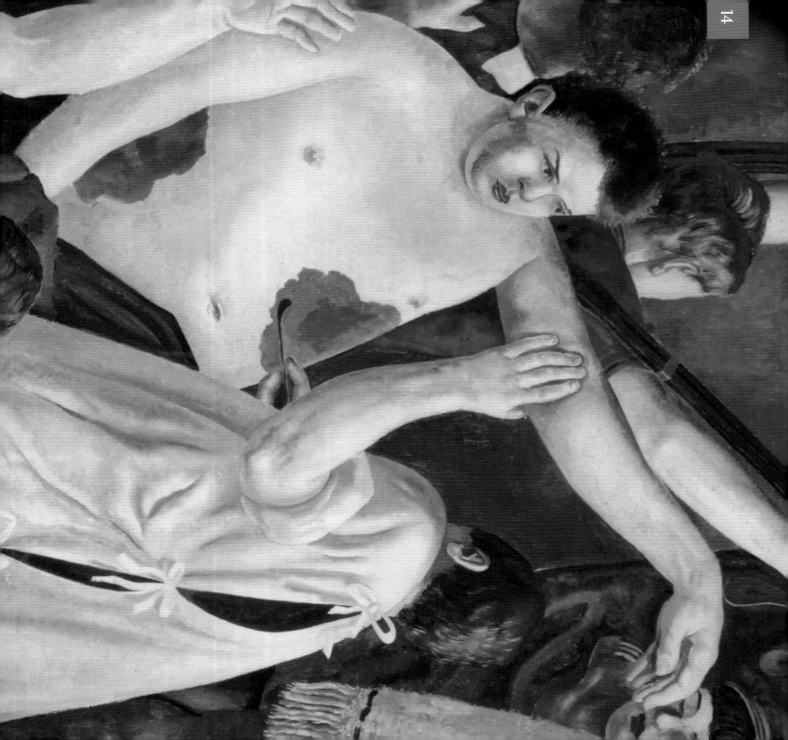

## 3 Ablutions

Soldiers wash and dry themselves in the Beaufort Hospital bathroom. In the centre, an orderly disinfects a chest wound with iodine. Two soldiers shampoo their hair, while a third vigorously polishes a tap with a towel, 'on which depends his week-end pass'. The sponge was painted from life with perfect realism. Equally illusionistic are the pools of water at the bottom right. In the cycle, the figures are drawn to the same scale, apart from in this picture, where they have been scaled up.

## 4 Sorting and Moving Kit-Bags

When soldiers arrived at Beaufort Hospital, their bags were piled up in the hospital courtyard, where those that weren't bed-bound would point out their bag to the orderlies, who would then carry them to the wards. Spencer also remembered that the bags were padlocked. The barred windows underline the grim institutional atmosphere. Like *Scrubbing the Floor* (2), this was painted in Hampstead in 1927, before Spencer moved to Burghclere.

| 18 | | | | 19 | | | |
|----|---|---|---|----|----|----|----|
| 1 | 5 | 7 | 9 | 10 | 12 | 14 | 16 |
| | 3 | | | | | | 17 |
| 2 | 6 | 8 | 11 | 13 | 15 | |
| 4 | | | | | | |

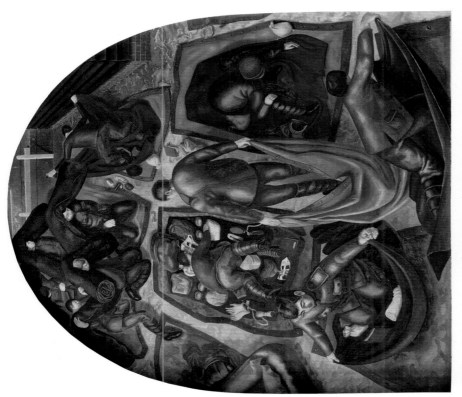

## 5 Kit Inspection

This is the only scene set at Tweseldown Camp near Farnham in Surrey, where Spencer was transferred from Beaufort Hospital for basic training before leaving for Macedonia. He was not a naturally tidy person, and must have struggled to lay out his kit on a ground sheet with the precision that military regulations demanded. Spencer's recollection of detail is astounding when one bears in mind that he was painting some ten years after the event. 'At the most important moments of my life I generally remember the least important facts.'

## 6 Sorting the Laundry

Spencer described the scene as follows: 'As each orderly called out the name of each article, the laundress would write it down in the respective orderly's "check-book".'. This is an energetic scene, with soldiers hurling clothes and sheets into the relevant pile. The interplay of colour (red and white) and texture is one that reappears in other canvases and gives a unity to the scheme as a whole. Spencer only painted two women in the cycle, one of whom is pictured here. The red and white spotted handkerchiefs belonged to the permanent inmates of Beaufort Hospital. The blue and white jackets are 'hospital blues', the uniform also seen in *Tea in the Hospital Ward* (13).

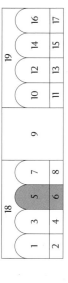

| 18 | | | | 19 | | | | |
|----|----|----|----|----|----|----|----|----|
| 1 | 3 | 5 | 7 | 9 | 10 | 12 | 14 | 16 |
| 2 | 4 | 6 | 8 | | 11 | 13 | 15 | 17 |

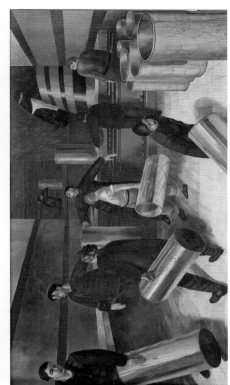

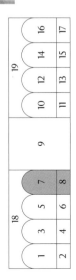

## 7 Dug-Out (or Stand-To)

*Dug-Out* is the first in the cycle to be set on the Salonika battle front in Macedonia. Men are about to put on their equipment, but have paused as they have become conscious of a change – the end of the war: 'It is a sort of cross between an "Armistice" picture and a "Resurrection".' This painting is a visual and conceptual introduction to the *Resurrection* altarpiece (9) on the end wall immediately to the right.

In a letter to Richard Carline in 1928, Spencer described this picture: 'The idea, apart from the way the shapes of the dug-outs interested me, occurred to me in thinking how marvellous it would be if one morning, when we came out of our dug-outs, we found that somehow everything was peace and that war was no more. That was one thing – the thought of how we would behave …'.

Spencer also described how the soldiers had to be ready for action at a moment's notice. Their equipment was laid out on the sides of the dug-outs so that when the order was given, they could put it on quickly.

## 8 Filling Tea Urns

The final predella (lower panel) scene on the north wall continues the hospital theme of the previous three. The tea urns were handled by the asylum inmates who worked in Beaufort Hospital. This predella was the only one placed in a different position from that indicated in Stanley's earlier sketch (now at the Stanley Spencer Gallery, Cookham). At the same time he decided to drop the scene showing a surgical operation, as he considered it too visceral. Spencer has paid particular attention to the reflection of the floor-tiles in the curved, polished-metal surface of the tea urns.

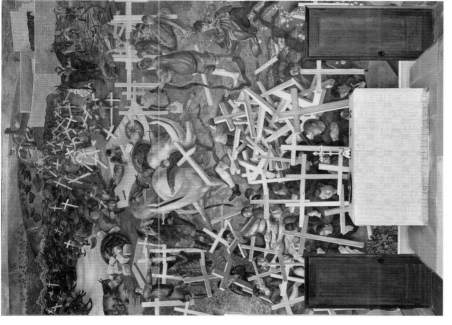

## 9 The Resurrection of the Soldiers

The *Resurrection* dominates the chapel, and all the other scenes are subordinate to it. The composition was the result of numerous preliminary sketches. It is based on a complex pattern of white-painted wooden crosses, which was suggested to Spencer by his habit of squaring up the canvas in order to scale up his design. As a living soldier hands in his rifle at the end of service, so a dead soldier carries his cross to Christ, who is seen in the middle distance receiving these crosses. Spencer's idea was that the cross produces a different reaction in everybody. As he explained, 'The truth that the cross is supposed to symbolise in this picture is that nothing is lost where a sacrifice has been the result of a perfect understanding … it very much influenced me in deciding the behaviour of the men'.

The central motif is a pair of dead mules, still harnessed to their timber wagon. Mules left a deep impression on Spencer and are a constant theme in his Macedonian pictures. Here the dead mules and their handler come back to life and turn towards the figure of Christ. On the wagon boards lies a young soldier intently studying his cross and the figure of Christ represented on it.

The foreground is related to the position of the altar and intended to form a subject in itself – 'a sort of portrait gallery formed by soldiers coming out of the ground and the crosses arranged so as to look like frames'. The soldiers are emerging from their graves behind the altar, shaking hands with their resurrected comrades.

The arched pictures and predellas could be painted on easels and took around 5–6 weeks. The *Resurrection* altarpiece was painted *in situ*, on canvas glued to the wall, and took nearly a year to complete. Spencer had to work on scaffolding erected by Bill Head the builder. He used a small wooden palette for both the easel and wall paintings. He chose not to wear overalls, preferring his tweed suit, which soon became splattered with paint.

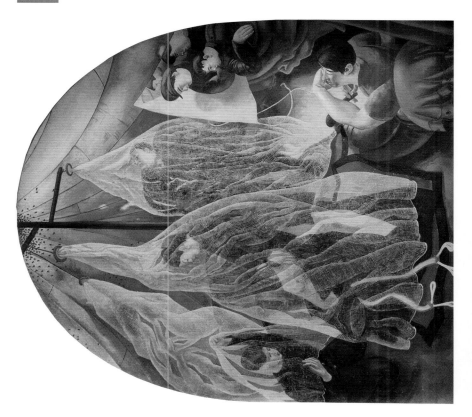

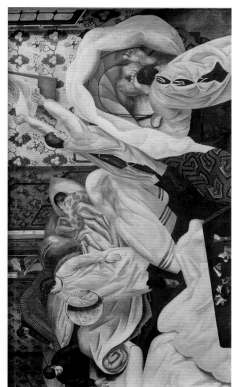

## 10 Reveille

*Reveille* is the early morning wake-up call. Such was the threat of malaria in Macedonia that soldiers were compelled to dress and undress under mosquito nets. Both Spencer and the dedicatee of the chapel, Henry Sandham, caught the disease. The way in which Spencer paints the nets is one of the most expressive passages of paint in the series. For Spencer this scene forms the final part of a triptych, with *Dug-Out* (7) and the big central *Resurrection* (9): 'a mixture of real and spiritual fact . . . the idea is again really the resurrection.' On the right, soldiers burst into the tent to announce to their comrades the resurrection and that the war is over.

## 11 Frostbite

This is another of the ward scenes set in Beaufort War Hospital. Again, all is busyness, as beds are made and mattresses turned. The floridly patterned wallpaper and carpet reinforce the mood. In the foreground an orderly inspects a patient's frostbitten feet. Scraping dead skin off patients' feet was one of the hospital jobs that Spencer had to do. Like malaria, frostbite was an affliction that could kill soldiers just as easily as an enemy bullet.

| 18 | | 19 | | | | |
|---|---|---|---|---|---|---|
| 1 | 3 | 5 | 7 | 9 | 10 | 12 | 14 | 16 |
| 2 | 4 | 6 | 8 | | 11 | 13 | 15 | 17 |

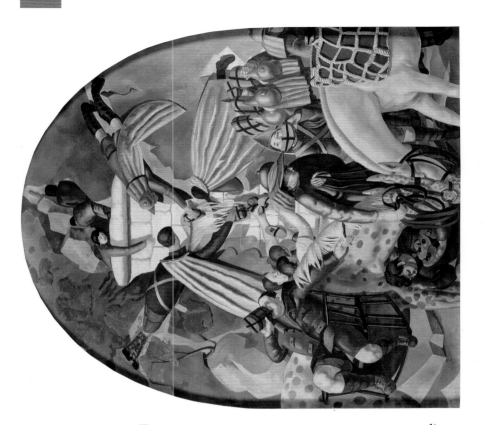

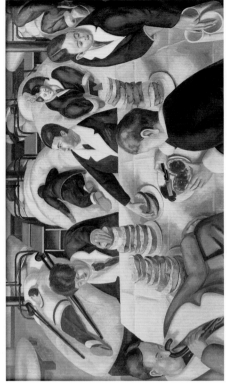

## 12 Filling Water-Bottles

Those fighting on the Salonika front had to endure heat as well as cold and malaria-infected insects. Here soldiers quench their thirst and fill their water bottles at a stream-fed fountain. Macedonia was the highlight of Spencer's wartime experiences. In depicting the everyday life of soldiers at war he managed to convey an element of mystery, even remoteness – in contrast to the mundane routine of hospital life. This is one of the last scenes that Spencer painted and reveals how his compositions became increasingly stylised during the course of the project, with the soldiers' mackintoshes forming a propeller-like shape.

## 13 Tea in the Hospital Ward

Food has always played an important part in hospital life, and Beaufort seems to have been no exception, if the tottering mounds of thickly buttered bread in this teatime scene are any indication. The focus of interest is the strawberry jam being lavishly spread on a slice – perhaps not surprisingly, as it was said to have been Spencer's favourite food. Not all are so interested: in the background, two patients sleep on their beds, while a third combs his hair. This scene did not feature in Spencer's original scheme and was one of the last of the predella canvases to be painted, in 1932.

| 18 | | | 19 | | | | |
|----|---|---|----|----|----|----|----|
| 1 | 3 | 5 | 7 | 9 | 10 | | 16 |
| | | | | | | 12 | 14 | 17 |
| 2 | 4 | 6 | 8 | | 11 | 13 | 15 | |

## 14 Map-reading

This is the only scene to depict an officer. He consults a map which records all the places Spencer could remember visiting in Macedonia. 'The map nearly fills the picture, with men, down below, resting on either side of the road. I loved this scene for the obvious reason of resting and contemplating.' The soldiers relax by picking bilberries, while the officer's horse feeds from a nose-bag. When painted in 1932, the officer and map were reduced in scale to conform with the scheme as a whole.

## 15 Bed-making

This bedroom scene is probably drawn from Spencer's memories of Beaufort Hospital and Macedonia, where he was a patient himself. The family photos pinned to the wall include: an early portrait of Hilda in the garden at Downshire Hill in Hampstead, as Spencer remembered her when they first met; one of his father in the porch of Hedsor Church, where he was organist; and Spencer's daughter Unity as a baby. This scene was not painted until 1932, when Spencer left Burghclere to live at Lindworth, Cookham.

| 18 | | | | 19 | | | |
|----|----|----|----|----|----|----|----|
| 1 | 3 | 5 | 7 | 9 | 10 | 12 | 16 |
| | | | | | 11 | 13 | 17 |
| 2 | 4 | 6 | 8 | | 14 | 15 | |

## 16 Firebelt

The grass is being burnt off round the camp to create a fire-break, using pages from the *Balkan News* as firelighters. The firelit night scene is probably the most technically accomplished in the entire cycle. He delighted in depicting the pattern created by the untethered guy-ropes of the tent, just as he had the soldiers' webbing in *Dug-Out* (7) and the braces in *Reveille* (10). Originally, Spencer had intended to paint soldiers playing cards in front of a camouflaged tent. This was the one of the last scenes to be painted, in 1932.

## 17 Washing Lockers

As part of the hygiene routine at Beaufort Hospital, the bedside lockers were regularly scrubbed in the bathroom of ward 4. Spencer was fascinated by the colour and shape of the bath-tubs. As he wrote in 1929: 'The baths were deep sort of magenta colour and shiny, and when you had a row of them end-view on, they looked marvellous.' Here, for a moment, he could achieve some precious time to himself: 'I have only mentally to place myself between the baths to feel at once inspired.'

| 18 | | | | 19 | | | | | | 16 |
|---|---|---|---|---|---|---|---|---|---|---|
| 1 | 3 | 5 | 7 | 9 | 10 | 12 | 14 | | | 17 |
| 2 | 4 | 6 | 8 | | 11 | 13 | 15 | | | |

## 18 Camp at Karasuli (North Wall)

The camp is shown in early morning. Men are cooking breakfast or carrying stones for the Serres military road, which winds through the background of the picture. Another man – Spencer himself – is collecting discarded copies of the *Balkan News*.

Spencer was employed at the 66th Field Ambulance in the camp at Karasuli, at first in the cookhouse: 'I would cook rashers for sixty men – two each ... As I knelt in a little groove cut in the ground for a wood fire, I had a wooden box full of cut rashers'.

## 19 Riverbed at Todorovo (South Wall)

In April 1917 Spencer moved to Todorovo, nearer the Bulgarian lines. The journey took eight days. Some of the soldiers are playing housey-housey, while others are making patterns out of pebbles, including, on the left, the badges of the Royal Army Medical Corps and the Royal Berkshires, the regiments in which Spencer served.

# Acknowledgements

Ann Danks, Carolyn Leder, Alison Paton, Sarah Rutherford. The new garden has been supported by a grant from the Heritage Lottery Fund.

© Maps in Minutes/Collins Bartholomew 2015

Ashdown House — Andover, Hungerford, Newbury, Wantage

Sandham Memorial Chapel — Kingsclere, Basingstoke, Whitchurch, Overton, Warngrove, Goring

Basildon Park — Reading, Earley

Greys Court — Henley-on-Thames

The Vyne — Whitchurch

West Green House Garden

# Bibliography

BEHREND, GEORGE, *Stanley Spencer at Burghclere*, London, 1965.

BELL, KEITH, *Stanley Spencer*, Royal Academy, 1980.

BRADLEY, AMANDA, AND HOWARD WATSON, ED., *Stanley Spencer: Heaven in a Hell of War*, Pallant House Gallery, 2013.

CARLINE, RICHARD, 'New Mural Paintings by Stanley Spencer', *Studio*, lxlvi, November 1928, pp.316–23.

CARLINE, RICHARD, *Stanley Spencer at War*, London, 1978.

COLLIS, MAURICE, *Stanley Spencer*, London, 1962.

GOUGH, PAUL, *Stanley Spencer: Journey to Burghclere*, Sansom & Co., Bristol, 2006.

GOUGH, PAUL, *Your Loving Friend, Stanley: The Great War Correspondence between Stanley Spencer and Desmond Chute*, Sansom & Co., Bristol, 2011.

POPLE, KENNETH, *Stanley Spencer*, London, 1991.

ROBINSON, DUNCAN, 'The Oratory of All Souls', *Stanley Spencer*, Arts Council, 1976.

ROBINSON, DUNCAN, *Stanley Spencer*, Oxford, 1979 [revised edition, 1990].

# Illustrations

All images © National Trust Images/John Hammond/Estate of Stanley Spencer/ Bridgeman Images, with the following exceptions: © Bridgeman Images/Brighton and Hove Museums/Estate of Henry Lamb 2015 p.8; © Bridgeman Images/Estate of Stanley Spencer 2015 p.3 (top right); © Glenside Museum, Bristol p.6; Imperial War Museum/Estate of Stanley Spencer 2015 p.5 (top left); © National Portrait Gallery/Estate of Henry Lamb 2015 p.4; National Trust Collections Management System no.790202 p.10 (bottom right); Alison Paton p.11; © Stanley Spencer Gallery, Cookham/ Estate of Stanley Spencer 2015 p.3 (bottom right); © Tate/Estate of Stanley Spencer 2015 p.5 (bottom right).

High-quality prints from the extensive and unique collections of National Trust Images are available at **www.ntprints.com**

**Thank you for buying this guidebook. Your support helps us look after places like this.**

# The Stanley Spencer Gallery, Cookham

The gallery is dedicated to the life and work of Cookham's most famous son, Stanley Spencer. It is located in the former Wesleyan chapel in Cookham High Street, which Spencer attended as a child with his mother. The permanent collection comprises over 100 paintings and drawings, and includes many long-term loans. The gallery puts on regular exhibitions of Spencer's work with the assistance of the Friends of the Stanley Spencer Gallery, a group of enthusiastic volunteers.

For opening times, admission charges and further details, see www.stanleyspencer.org.uk.

# The National Trust

is a registered charity is independent of government

was founded in 1895 to preserve places of historic interest or natural beauty permanently for the benefit of the nation

relies on the generosity of its supporters, through membership subscriptions, gifts, legacies and the contribution of many tens of thousands of volunteers

protects and opens to the public over 350 historic houses, gardens and parks, ancient monuments and nature reserves

owns around 250,000 hectares (618,000 acres) of the most beautiful countryside and 775 miles of outstanding coastline for people to enjoy.

If you would like to become a member or make a donation, please telephone 0344 800 1895 (minicom 0344 800 4410); write to National Trust, PO Box 574, Manvers, Rotherham S63 3FH; alternatively, see our website at **www.nationaltrust.org.uk**

© 2015 The National Trust

Reprinted 2017

Registered charity number 205846

ISBN 978-1-84359-469-7

Text by Amanda Bradley

Edited by Oliver Garnett

Designed by Blacker Design

Printed by Park Lane Press, Corsham for National Trust (Enterprises) Ltd, Heelis, Kemble Drive, Swindon, Wilts SN2 2NA on Cocoon Silk made from 100% recycled paper

Opposite Detail of *Kit Inspection* (5)